I0468221

ACCOUNTING OUTSOURCING SERVICES

Facts every small business owners should know before outsource their accounting work

By

AINI AMAN

PREFACE

This book is useful for you as a business owner, manager or executive who are thinking to outsource your accounting work to third party service providers.

Before deciding to outsource your accounting work, you must know what is accounting outsourcing, why you need to outsource your accounting, how to do it right, who and where you should outsource your accounting work to. This book will provide you with answers to those questions to ensure that all the process and activities of accounting outsourcing are properly implemented.

Despite outsourcing your accounting work to the same location, you can choose to outsource your accounting work to other countries that provide low operational cost such as India, China and Malaysia. Where is the best location to outsource your accounting work?

Again, this book is useful for you who intend to outsource your accounting work to service provider. This book will reveal things that you should consider and help you to take control of your accounting work even though it is done by third party.

TABLE OF CONTENTS

1. WHAT IS ACCOUNTING OUTSOURCING?

Outsourcing refers to an initiative in which a company appoints a third party to conduct a work or be an expertise in their company. It is the process of transferring responsibility of specific business function from a group of employees of the company to another group of employees in another company (external) based on a contractual agreement for a specific period.

Accounting outsourcing refer to the use of third parties service providers to process your accounting transactions. You could outsource your accounting processes that has high level of transactions such as collecting debt, invoicing clients, paying service providers, filing tax and paying staff salaries. You could also send more complex accounting work such as financial planning, tax strategy and budgeting depending on your business needs.

Accounting processes can be either outsourced externally to third party service providers or outsourced internally to another subsidiary in the same company (also known as accounting shared services).

THIRD PARTY ACCOUNTING OUTSOURCING

Companies generally prefer to outsource their accounting work to third party service provider for the following reasons, mainly to:

- obtain new technology, skills and knowledge

- improve business processes and enable change in the company

- provide short-term service needs without involving an increase in overall operating costs

- acquire internal resources for strategic planning

If you outsource your full accounting process to third party accounting service providers, you only need to pass your accounting related documents to the service provider. The service provider will record your accounting transaction and prepare your company's financial statements. If you like, you could strategically outsource the whole accounting function to third party service provider so that you could focus on your core business.

Most businesses such as the sole trader, partnership, private limited companies, middle market companies or multinational companies have already outsource their accounting to third party service providers mainly for the preparation of financial statement, audit and tax. Government bodies and its agencies send part of their accounting related work to third party service providers. This include payroll and procurement. Non-profit organization such as public higher education, welfare organizations and religious communities typically also send their accounting work to third party service provider.

ACCOUNTING SHARED SERVICES

Accounting Shared Services Center (SSC) is a separate entity established within the company to handle accounting related work for all subsidiaries. This is sometimes called as internal outsourcing. Costs can be saved when all activities like billing, accounts payable, management and processing of travel claims and expenses are managed using the same resources in the SSC.

Companies choose to outsource internally, mainly because they want to:

- obtain full control over major projects
- minimize the risk of outsourcing
- provide professional development for staff
- use existing expertise

- manage changes in the contract and coordination

- facilitate control over costs

- minimize cost for the necessary services

- has ownership and control over resources and personal assets of the company

If you choose to establish SSC, you need to have certain expertise to perform services or activities. You have to really know your accounting operation, related costs and time required for SSC implementation. Accounting SSC implementation generally involved the following costs:

- cost of full time and additional staff

- overtime cost to carry out the SSC project

- opportunity cost if the SSC does not meet the desired project outcome.

The decision to establish shared services is based on the best use of companies' resources and depending on their needs and priorities. For example, a bank known as IBG (pseudonym) set up its Shared Service Center called IPS (also a pseudonym) to ensure that it can focus on core banking activities, while maintaining the confidentiality of customers' information. Accounting services provided by IPS to the bank include credit process, trial balance process, check clearance, credit card processing, automobile loans processing, electronic banking, payment processing and financial report. Accounting work which is conducted in the SSC still requires high level management from the bank to ensure the accuracy of accounting records.

In short, accounting outsourcing refers to the transfer of accounting work such as general accounting, tax or financial management to third party accounting service providers or shared service center.

2. WHY ACCOUNTING OUTSOURCING?

You need to know four main reasons that make companies chose to outsource their accounting work to accounting service providers.

COST SAVINGS

First is cost savings. This is the main reason that made most companies choose accounting outsourcing. Cost saving is usually reported between 20-50%. For example, Rhodia, a manufacturer of chemical products reveal a cost saving of 30% within two years after outsource its accounting work. Most small and medium-sized businesses who choose to use the accounting outsourcing services achieve cost savings around 50%.

Where is the cost savings come from? It is mainly due to the restructuring of your fixed costs and variable costs; saving labor costs, space rental and other management costs. The use of accounting outsourcing services will allow the movement of fixed cost to variable cost and allow variable costs to be more predictable. For instance, when you use accounting outsourcing services, your accounting related management cost will be transferred to the third party. You do not have to worry about hiring, training or paying your account executives or account clerks anymore. All of this costs will be transferred to your accounting service provider.

In addition to the savings in labor costs, you could save other management cost such as the use of paper, as most of reporting and communication process in accounting outsourcing is usually carried out online. Rental spaces that are typically used for accounts department can be eliminated. You could also use the space for other services that can contribute to additional revenue to your company.

FOCUS ON CORE ACTIVITIES

Second is focus on core activities. Accounting outsourcing allows you as the business owner to devote significant resources such as investment, labor, infrastructure as well as your valuable time to your core business activities. For example, payroll processing is not your core business activity but you have to manage it anyway. You could outsource your payroll processing and focus your available resources to produce goods of higher quality and be more competitive.

We know that the accounting work such as payment, billing, cash collection and distribution of revenue is relatively routine, detailed and require full attention. If the accounting work is outsource, your financial manager could focus his time and energy on financial analysis, budgeting, forecasting and strategic planning that can help improve your company performance.

SKILLED WORKERS

Third is skilled workers. Accounting work requires a person with certain qualification and skills that you need to pay high salary if you are looking for a good accountant. An average salary for an accountant in the United States is $18.63 per hour or $47,936 annually. With the price of $47,936 annually, you can cover for at least one accounting operation center in India!

In addition, with accounting outsourcing services, you can gain access to accounting experts which are scarce and expensive at a reasonable cost. With accounting outsourcing, there will be no further delays in entering data or journal transaction records until the end of the year. The service provider will complete the work on a daily basis, which will save overtime costs. This will facilitate and expedite the preparation of financial statements and audit work.

COMPLIANCE TO ACCOUNTING ACT

Fourth is compliance to Accounting Act. The cost to non-compliance to Accounting Act is expensive. It could damage your company's image and reduce investor confidence. For example, Sarbanes-Oxley Act 2002 stipulates that all CEOs and CFOs have to be responsible to ensure that their corporate financial information is complete and accurate.

Regardless of your company size, you need an accountant to manage your accounting to ensure that your company profitability is recorded accurately. Even a slightest mistake such as a mistake of entering data into accounting system will have a significant impact on the preparation of the year-end statements. Experts of the accounting service provider usually have deep knowledge in a complex tax calculation, reporting policy and reporting period. They will make sure that your financial report are complied with the required Accounting Act. The accounting outsourcing service providers can also help you in your tax preparation so you are not overpaid or underpaid your taxes.

In short, companies outsource their accounting work for various reasons. It could be because of cost, skilled workers, focus on core activities or compliance to Accounting Act.

3. WHO SHOULD BE YOUR ACCOUNTING OUTSOURCING SERVICE PROVIDER?

Now that you feel like you have a reason to outsource your accounting work but you are not sure which accounting outsourcing service provider to choose. There are only two choices: accounting firm or non-accounting firm.

ACCOUNTING FIRM

Big players in accounting outsourcing in the industry is made up of a large accounting firm namely KPMG, Ernst & Young LLP, and Deloitte & Touche Tohmatsu. Accounting outsourcing has long flourished as a major source of revenue for the accounting firms. The large accounting firms provide high level of accounting services such as assurance, tax, financial advisory and IT outsourcing consultancy for medium and large size companies. On the other hand, small accounting firms provide accounting services on a small scale and focus on small and medium size companies. The type of accounting services provided can be ranged from basic bookkeeping to a complete preparation of financial statement.

NON-ACCOUNTING FIRM

Other than accounting firms, there are non-accounting firms that provide accounting outsourcing services. Non-accounting firms hired accounting experts to perform accounting work for their clients. For example, Accenture is one of the leaders in the field of consulting, technology and accounting outsourcing in the world. They have the experience and ability in a variety of industries and functional business that they could provide accounting outsourcing services to their customers throughout their centers around the world. Its main operations are located in the United States and across Europe, Middle East and Africa.

IT outsourcing firms often include accounting services for their clients. They offer added value services that include management accounting network, accounting systems analysis, budgeting system, accounting information systems, inventory management systems and strategic management analysis. The IT outsourcing firm also assists in developing expertise in certain fields such as business software, technology development, information technology infrastructure management, systems integration, information assurance, knowledge management, system software development, data operations, facility management and management consulting.

FREELANCER

You can also save yourself time by outsourcing the more accounting tasks to an experienced freelancer. The service that the freelancer can provide will be bespoke based on your requirements. The freelancer focus solely on the financial statements and do all day to day work as well as year-end compliance work. This often extends beyond book-keeping or accounts production to also include the issuing of invoices and associated record keeping.

In short, you do not have to outsource your accounting work to big accounting firm. Although the accounting provide high value of accounting work, it can be expensive for many reasons. There are non-accounting firm, IT outsourcing firm or a freelancer who could assist you with various type of accounting and bookkeeping services at reasonable costs.

4. What You Need To Consider When Making Decision For Accounting Outsourcing?

Before outsourcing your accounting work, you should conduct four assessments to ensure a sound outsourcing decision.

Evaluate Your Business Activities

First, evaluate your business activities. If you plan to use accounting outsourcing, you must first determine whether or not your accounting function is your business core activities. Usually, only non-core business activities are outsourced. Companies that succeed in outsourcing activities often have a clear understanding on their core activities. They also has extensive planning and clear goals for accounting outsourcing. For example, they outsourced their accounting work in order to reduce operation cost and focus on core business activities.

For example, DEPRO Tech outsourced its accounting work since it had difficulties to hire an accountant and at the same time, the CEO felt that they should focus on company's mission and core activities.

EVALUATE YOUR VALUE CHAIN ACTIVITIES

Second, evaluate your value chain activities. Value chain analysis is a useful tool for working out how you can create the greatest possible value to your customers. The more value you create, the more your customer are willing to pay. Value chain analysis involves three important steps. First, you need to identify the activities you have to undertake to deliver your services. Second, for each activity you need to think through what you would do to add the greatest value for your customer. Thirdly, you need to evaluate which of the process do not add value for your customers but you need to do it to get sustain your business. This is the process that you should outsource. For example, invoicing is not a core activity to a catering services but you have to do it to get payment from your client. That is why, invoice processing is usually sent for accounting outsourcing.

EVALUATE YOUR COST

Third, evaluate the cost that might be involved if you outsource your accounting work. You have to try your best to provide the most accurate cost estimate, the length of time and opportunity costs that might be involved. The decision to outsource your accounting work usually starts with a plan which identify all the costs associated with outsourcing activities. You should get a quote form few companies to find the most competitive one. If the service provider is picked solely on cost, it may not be qualified to provide certain services and, in turn, you will not receive the right service or advice on time.

EVALUATE YOUR POTENTIAL SERVICE PROVIDER

Fourth, evaluate your service provider. Instead of only looking for a low cost service provider, you must carefully assess the offerings, requisite skills, experience and capabilities of potential service providers. The best way to evaluate a prospective service provider is to examine their service track record from multiple perspective. You need to find out how accounting work will be managed, who will be the account manager for your work.

If possible, you need to request for information related to their infrastructure, technology partners, internet providers, data centers, network environment and key metrics. Nevertheless, a good relationship with your accounting service providers need to be supported by the trust in the relationship, in addition to contract signed and agreed by both parties.

In short, there are four evaluations that you need to make before making decision to outsource or not: evaluate your business activities, value chain, costs and potential service providers.

5. What You Need Do To Ensure Smooth Transition?

Once you made a decision to outsource your accounting work to the potential service provider, you need to perform four important steps to ensure smooth transition.

Request For Proposal

First, you need to issue an open tender (refer to RFP-Request for Proposal) as an invitation to the third-party provider. Usually through a bidding process, the service provider will send the paperwork over a particular service. Bidding process is the best method in the negotiation of the company and shows the purchasing power with service providers. The request will lead to the formation of risk exposure and the results and benefits that will exist in identifying the best service provider for your company. Service providers who do not qualify will be excluded from the list so that only a few are left. Usually it occurs at the level of due diligence where only two service providers would compete at this level. You can then ask to submit their best and final offer (Best and Final

Offer or BAFO), from which you make a final selection.

NEGOTIATE CONTRACT

Second, after you choose your accounting service provider, you can start negotiate a contract. This negotiation will take the original proposals (Request for Proposal or RFP). At this stage, any related documents and price of the services will be determined. The service provider are selected based on the terms agreed in the contract.

The contract contains list of agreed items such as information management, benchmarking, control, intellectual property, data security, access rights information, data confidentiality, and accountability. Some contract emphasis on service penalties, procedural improvements, size, profit sharing, penalties and liabilities as well as provision of resources for the early termination of a contract.

What is important in any outsourcing agreement is a contractual agreement that defines how you and service providers will work. This is a formal legal document, which become the basis for the governance of a relationship. There are three important dates that you need to be aware: (1) the date the contract is signed, (2) the effective date on which the terms of the contract will be activated, and

(3) the date of service will be started or the date the service provider will take over the service.

PLAN FOR TRANSITION PROCESS

Third, after the contract is signed, the next step is to negotiate with service providers on a number of things to ensure the transition process went smoothly. The transition here means moving the functional or internal activities to the service provider. The important thing to consider are the reengineering of your internal processes: establishing formal groups dedicated to the assigned activities, moving staff to other parts of the company or to the provider, appointing individuals responsible for the outsourcing, holding periodic assessment, and making arrangements in the event of layoffs.

ASSESS YOUR SERVICE PROVIDER

Fourth, you need to make an assessment of accounting outsourcing activities that are carried out. Among the things that should be considered is the efficiency and effectiveness of the accounting work provided by the chosen service provider. You need to assess whether the quality of outsourcing and outsourcing would be as agreed in the contract.

Reassessment of your relationship with service provider should start from the date of implementation of outsourcing and should continue for at least four months. This is an assignment or transfer process to determine which employees will be assigned to the project. It also involves a process of transformation where the emphasis is on standardization and centralization. At this stage of risk analysis is also performed to assess the types of risk that may be encountered when using outsourcing.

In short, you really need to plan your accounting outsourcing by taking into consideration the bidding, contract negotiation, transitions plan and assessment process. Next, a few months before the contract expires, a decision should be made whether to terminate or renew the contract. Termination of the contract may involve taking back service (internal party would run alone) or move it to the outsourcing provider to another.

6. What You Need To Consider At The End Of Your Accounting Outsourcing Contract?

At the end of the contract period, the service provider's performance will be assessed from periodic reports that are available. If the performance is not satisfactory, you outsourcing company can decide whether to cancel the contract immediately, withdraw some of the outsourcing or pull-back overall activities of accounting outsourcing. There are five steps that you need to consider to address at the end of your accounting outsourcing contract.

Understand Outsourcing Procedure

First, you need to understand the outsourcing procedures on contract withdrawal. If you decide to withdraw at the end of contract period, you should be ready to deal with service providers who will find ways to delay, prevent, or otherwise request a payment appropriate to their tasks. For example, DEPRO Tech decided to withdraw its accounting work from service provider at the end of the contract. One of the reasons was the performance of the service provider did not meet their expectation. Some of the common problems that often occur include errors and mistakes in reported assets and expenses, delays in completing reports and errors in classifying assets. Despite that, the service provider felt that the company was not ready to take back their accounting work and try to negotiate and renew the contract.

DECIDE ON WITHDRAWAL

Second, after assessing outsourcing procedures, decisions about how and when to perform withdrawal involves determining whether to implement it in stages or all at once. Reducing outsourcing work in stages will enable both parties to make the necessary adjustments and preparations. For example, when DEPRO decided to terminate the contract on 31 December 2007, they took almost a year to exactly terminate the outsourcing work. DEPRO extended the contract for another year to ensure smooth transition of accounting work from service provider. However, there is a potential risk where your outsourcing service providers would probably provide less service quality during the extended period of the contract.

DEVELOP WITHDRAWAL PLAN

Third, you need to develop withdrawal plan is an important action to withdrawal. Commitment from top management is crucial at this stage. Planning should include areas such as data transfer and ownership system, recruitment, purchase of equipment and software as well as a space to be allocated. Planning to implement the withdrawal covers two main sources: accounting systems and staff expertise.

WITHDRAWAL TRANSITION PLAN

Fourth, the withdrawal transition plan should consist the following:

- Principles under which the transition will be conducted.

- Document each party's disengagement responsibilities.

- Outline the areas to be included in the finalized plan.

- Specify the data sources required to finalize the plan.

- Propose high-level work breakdown structures describing in more detail the broad deliverables.

At this stage, you may want to consider defining a reasonable and appropriate fee structure for termination assistance services. These fees should reflect the service providers' costs and should be paid upon successful completion of transition process. However, if your service provider has triggered termination through breach of agreement, fees should be determined differently.

Continuous Assessment

Fifth, once the withdrawal is agreed, the activities previously delivered to the service provider will be managed by your company. However, the process will not be as easy as you thought. It is therefore very important for you to continuous assess the effectiveness of this function.

The post-withdrawal period is a complex and difficult process. It involves the preparation and implementation of plans of your company and service providers, limited finances and insufficient expertise, unforeseen and uncontrollable factors, and service provider collaboration.

In short, withdrawal is a common method to define the functional recovery of business activity that was previously transferred to accounting outsourcing service providers. It is important for you to develop specific plan for withdrawal that should include the five aspects; assessment of the existing outsourcing procedures, deciding whether to terminate, reduce or withdrawal, developing plans for withdrawal, transition withdrawal, solution withdrawal and continuous evaluation.

7. MOVING FORWARD

What else needs to be done to ensure smooth accounting outsourcing process? The involvement of all parties is important. It is not only limited to the involvement of the service providers but also your own involvement.

This book has disclosed facts that you as a business owner should know when trying to outsource your accounting work. By now, you have basic understanding on accounting outsourcing, reasons for outsourcing, accounting service providers, decision making, implementation and withdrawal processes.

Nevertheless, globalization and liberalization of world poses some implications for accounting outsourcing services industry. The challenge of globalization has created pressure on accounting outsourcing service providers to be more competitive locally and globally. It is important to take into consideration factors discussed in this book when searching for accounting service provider who can offer services at low costs but with good quality.

These facts are very important to be aware of to ensure the success of any outsourcing activities. It is hoped that this book will provide some guidance and illustration important to the management of the company before making a decision with regard to outsourcing. Despite the facts highlighted in this book, there are other potential risks in accounting outsourcing that you need to evaluate and mitigate. I will discuss further on such challenges in my next book. Stay tune!

ABOUT THE AUTHOR

About The Author

Aini Aman (Dr.) has almost 15 years research experience in Finance & Accounting Shared Services and Outsourcing. Her research started since 2001. To date, she had successfully managed more than RM2 million research grants in the above areas. Her latest research project is establishing Impact Sourcing initiatives, working with government and Industry and developing Global Shared Service Courses to develop talent pool in the Shared Services and Outsourcing Industry. In addition she produced case studies for Integrated Case Studies course and Entrepreneurship training, books and articles for journal publications.

Find out more at http://www.amazon.com/author/ainiaman

Other Books at Amazon.com

Accounting Outsourcing Services
Communicating Knowledge in Offshore Software
Development

Coming soon…

Global Business Services: Introduction
Global Business Services: Governance & Reporting
Global Business Services: Risks & Control
Global Business Services: Project Management
Global Business Services: Team Management
Global Business Services: Talent Management
Global Business Services: Disruptive Technology
Global Business Services: Finance & Accounting
Global Business Services: Information Technology
Global Business Services: Human Resources
Global Business Services: Big Data Analytics
Global Business Services: Selected Case Studies

Can I Ask a Favour?

If you enjoyed this book, found it useful or otherwise then I'd really appreciate it if you would post a short review on Amazon. I do read all the reviews personally so that I can continually write what people are wanting.

Thanks for your support!